GIANT OCEAN ANIMALS

ORCA

Clever Predator

BY EMMANUEL MARSHALL

Enslow PUBLISHING

Please visit our website, www.enslow.com. For a free color catalog of all our high-quality books, call toll free 1-800-398-2504 or fax 1-877-980-4454.

Cataloging-in-Publication Data
Names: Marshall, Emmanuel.
Title: Orca / Emmanuel Marshall.
Description: Buffalo, NY : Enslow Publishing, 2027. | Series: Giant ocean animals | Includes glossary and index.
Identifiers: ISBN 9781978550742 (pbk.) | ISBN 9781978550759 (library bound) | ISBN 9781978550766 (ebook)
Subjects: LCSH: Killer whale--Juvenile literature.
Classification: LCC QL737.C432 M377 2027 | DDC 599.536--dc23

Published in 2027 by
Enslow Publishing
2544 Clinton Street
Buffalo, NY 14224

Portions of this work were originally authored by Angela Lim and published as *Orcas*. All new material in this edition was authored by Emmanuel Marshall.

Cover Designer: Joshua Olson
Interior Designer: Joshua Olson
Editor: Noah Riccardi

Photo Credits: Cover, p. 1 Christian Musat/Shutterstock.com; pp. 4–5, 18–19 Tory Kallman/Shutterstock.com; pp. 6–7 Ken Canning/iStockphoto; pp. 8, 22–23 sethakan/iStockphoto; p. 9 Foto 4440/Shutterstock.com; pp. 10–11, 29 vladsilver/iStockphoto; pp. 12–13 ca2hill/iStockphoto; pp. 14–15 Michael Zeigler/iStockphoto; pp. 16–17 Will Falcon/Shutterstock.com; pp. 20–21 Mark Malleson/iStockphoto; pp. 24–25 Rasmus-Raahauge/iStockphoto; p. 26 Tobias Brehm/Shutterstock.com; p. 27 Konstantin39/Shutterstock.com.

Printed in China

CPSIA compliance information: Batch #QS27ENS: For further information contact Enslow Publishing, at 1-800-398-2504.

TABLE OF CONTENTS

CHAPTER 1

DEADLY DOLPHINS

Orcas are large dolphins. They are fierce **predators** that hunt many animals for food. Orcas are fast swimmers. They can reach speeds of 28 miles per hour (45 km/h) or more.

Orcas can sometimes jump out of the water.

Orcas' dorsal fins often stick up above the water.

Orcas can grow up to 32 feet (9.8 m) long. And they can weigh more than 13,000 pounds (5,900 kg).

A male orca's dorsal fin can be about 6 feet (2 m) tall.

Orcas are famous for the black-and-white patterns on their skin. Under their skin, they have thick layers of fat. This fat helps keep orcas warm in cold waters.

Water sprays from an orca's blowhole as it breathes.

An orca hunts for seals by the shore.

SNEAK ATTACK

An orca's black-and-white skin blends in with dark waters. That makes the orca hard for animals to spot. It can sneak up on its **prey**.

CHAPTER 2

AROUND THE WORLD

Orcas live in every ocean around the world. Some live near the North Pole. Others live close to the South Pole.

Some orcas have lived for more than 90 years.

Tourists watch an orca from their boat.

An orca sleeps with one eye open.

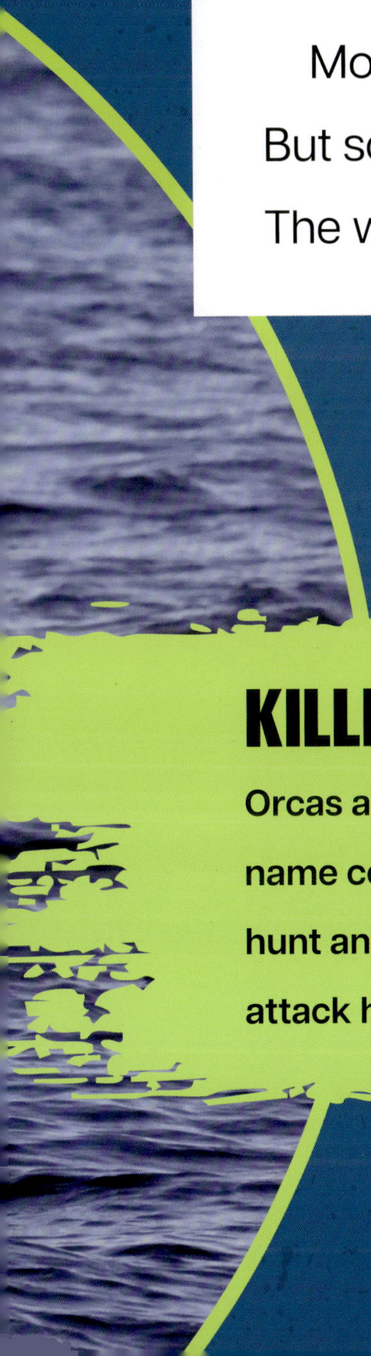

Most orcas live in cold waters. But some swim near the **equator**. The water is warmer there.

KILLER OF WHALES

Orcas are sometimes called killer whales. The name comes from early sailors. They saw orcas hunt and kill whales. Orcas almost never attack humans.

Orcas travel in groups called pods. The orcas in a pod swim and hunt together. Some pods **migrate**. They follow their prey. Other pods stay in the same area.

A pod of orcas dive in the blue ocean.

Orcas don't have a sense of smell.

CHAPTER 3

FAMILY MATTERS

About 40 orcas make up a pod. These orcas live together their whole lives. The oldest female leads the group.

Pods of orcas can travel long distances.

Sometimes several pods join together. Orcas often find **mates** this way. Females give birth to one baby at a time.

Orcas come up to the water's surface to breathe.

Newborn orcas have slightly pink parts of their bodies.

CHATTY GROUPS

Orca pods **communicate** with one another. They whistle. Each pod makes **unique** sounds. That way, members recognize one another.

A young orca swims next to its mother.

Pods of orcas are like families. Older orcas teach young ones. These young orcas learn to hunt and communicate. They also learn migration paths.

An orca can eat hundreds of pounds of food in a single day.

CHAPTER 4

BRAINS AND BRAWN

Orcas hunt a wide variety of animals. They often eat fish, seals, and sharks. Orcas are known for their hunting tactics. They have many clever ways of hunting prey.

Some orcas eat seabirds.

Orcas use sounds to find food. They make clicking sounds. The sounds bounce off fish. These **echoes** reveal where the fish are. This process is known as echolocation.

Orcas work together to hunt fish.

An orca's teeth can be 4 inches (10 cm) long.

Sometimes orcas use waves to hunt. Several orcas splash a wave onto a piece of floating ice. The wave can wash seals off the ice and into the water.

Orcas often try to hunt seals that are resting on ice.

Orcas are the only natural predators of great white sharks.

MORE WAYS TO HUNT

To catch prey, orcas sometimes blow bubbles. This traps fish near the ocean's surface. Other times, orcas attack sharks. They flip a shark onto its back. That way, the shark can't swim away.

TEST YOUR KNOWLEDGE

Take this quiz to test your knowledge.

1. Write a sentence that describes the main idea of Chapter 3.

2. Orcas have many ways of hunting prey. Which was your favorite to learn about? Why?

3. What do orcas use to find food?

    A. sounds
    B. smells
    C. sunlight

4. How would blending in with the water help orcas catch prey?

    A. They could not swim as fast as their prey.
    B. They could swim far from prey without making noise.
    C. They could swim closer to prey without being seen.

5. What does **fierce** mean in this book?

They are ***fierce*** *predators that hunt many animals for food.*

- **A.** slow and old
- **B.** small and weak
- **C.** strong and smart

6. What does **tactics** mean in this book?

Orcas are known for their hunting ***tactics****. They have many clever ways of hunting prey.*

- **A.** weapons for fighting
- **B.** smart ways to do a task
- **C.** wrong ways to do a task

Answers can be found on page 32.

GLOSSARY

communicate
To send and receive messages.

dorsal
Located on the back.

echoes
Sounds that have bounced off a surface.

equator
An invisible line that runs around the middle of Earth.

mates
Pairs of animals that come together to have babies.

migrate
To move from one part of the world to another.

predators
Animals that hunt and eat other animals.

prey
An animal that is hunted and eaten by another animal.

unique
Different from all others.

FOR MORE INFORMATION

BOOKS

Murray, Julie. *Orcas*. Minneapolis, MN: Abdo Publishing, 2025.

Peters, Katie. *Swimming Orcas*. Minneapolis, MN: Lerner Publications, 2025.

WEBSITES

Britannica Kids: Killer Whale

kids.britannica.com/kids/article/killer-whale/574601

Learn more about killer whales, which is another name for orcas.

National Geographic Kids: Orca

kids.nationalgeographic.com/animals/mammals/facts/orca

Learn more about orcas at this website.

Publisher's note to educators and parents: Our editors have carefully reviewed these websites to ensure that they are suitable for students. Many websites change frequently, however, and we cannot guarantee that a site's future contents will continue to meet our high standards of quality and educational value. Be advised that students should be closely supervised whenever they access the internet.

INDEX

Answer Key:
1. Answers will vary; 2. Answers will vary; 3. A; 4. C; 5. C; 6. B